# KOBE BRYANT

## NBA SCORING SENSATION

CONNOR DAYTON

**Britannica**
Educational Publishing

IN ASSOCIATION WITH

**ROSEN**
EDUCATIONAL SERVICES

Published in 2016 by Britannica Educational Publishing (a trademark of Encyclopædia Britannica, Inc.) in association with The Rosen Publishing Group, Inc.

29 East 21st Street, New York, NY 10010

Distributed exclusively by Rosen Publishing.

To see additional Britannica Educational Publishing titles, go to rosenpublishing.com.

First Edition

**Britannica Educational Publishing**

J.E. Luebering: Director, Core Reference Group

Anthony L. Green, Editor, Compton's by Britannica

**Rosen Publishing**

Hope Kilcoyne: Executive Editor

Amelie von Zumbusch: Editor

Nelson Sá: Art Director

Nicole Russo: Designer

Cindy Reiman: Photography Manager

**Library of Congress Cataloging-in-Publication Data**

Dayton, Connor.

Kobe Bryant: NBA scoring sensation/Connor Dayton.—First Edition.

     pages cm.—(Living legends of sports)

Includes bibliographical references and index.

ISBN 978-1-68048-109-9 (library bound)—ISBN 978-1-68048-110-5 (pbk.)—ISBN 978-1-68048-112-9 (6-pack)

1. Bryant, Kobe, 1978-—Juvenile literature. 2. Basketball players—United States—Biography—Juvenile literature. 3. Los Angeles Lakers (Basketball team)—Juvenile literature. I. Title.

GV884.B794D38 2016

796.332092—dc23

[B]

2014039768

*Manufactured in the United States of America*

**Photo credits:** Cover, p. 1 Andy Lyons/Getty Images; p. 4 Stephen Dunn/Getty Images; pp. 7 © 2000 NBA Entertainment. Photo by Andrew D. Bernstein/NBAE/Getty Images; p. 9 Frank Ramspott/Digital Vision Vectors/Getty Images; p. 11 Al Tielemans/Sports Illustrated/Getty Images; p.12 © 1996 NBA Entertainment. Photo by Nathaniel S. Butler/ NBAE/Getty Images; p. 15 © AP Images; p. 16 © 1998 NBA Entertainment. Photo by Andrew D. Bernstein/NBAE/Getty Images; p.18 © 2006 NBA Entertainment. Photo by Andrew D. Bernstein/NBAE/Getty Images; p. 19 New York Daily News Archive/Getty Images; pp. 20–21 © 2004 NBA Entertainment. Photo by Juan Ocampo /NBAE/Getty Images; p. 23 © 2006 NBA Entertainment. Photo by Noah Graham/NBAE/Getty Images; p. 24 © 2008 NBA Entertainment. Photo by Noah Graham/NBAE/Getty Images; p. 27 Sacramento Bee/McClatchy-Tribune/Getty Images; pp. 28–29 Fort Worth Star-Telegram/McClatchy-Tribune/Getty Images; p. 31 Christian Petersen/Getty Images; p. 32 The Boston Globe/Getty Images; p. 33 Greg Nelson/Sports Illustrated/Getty Images; p. 34 © 2013 NBA Entertainment. Photo by Fernando Medina/NBAE/Getty Images; p. 37 Chip Somodevilla/Getty Images; p. 38 Barry King/FilmMagic/Getty Images; p. 39 Scott Halleran/Getty Images; cover and interior pages background images © iStockphoto.com/block37 (basketball court illustration), © iStockphoto.com/ Nikada (texture).

# CONTENTS

# INTRO-
# DUCTION

**K**obe Bryant is a shooting guard for the Los Angeles Lakers. He has played for the team since 1996, when he entered the NBA straight from high school. It is rare for a player to be physic-ally developed and mature enough to handle the pressure of going pro at such a young age, but Bryant was up to the challenge.

Bryant is a talented ath-lete, but he works hard to push himself to record-breaking greatness. Throughout his career, he

Kobe Bryant *(left)* drives against Andre Iguodala of the Golden State Warriors during a November 2014 game.

has maintained a high shooting percentage. He has said that is because he does not practice *taking* shots at the hoop, he practices *making* them. This statement is just one example of his competitive nature!

Bryant consistently shows a laserlike focus on the game, no matter what injuries or personal problems he is facing. When he is in his "zone" and playing the sport he loves, everything else takes a back seat. There is no room for doubt or fear of failure. He says, "If you're afraid to fail, then you're probably going to fail."

Bryant's hard work has shown itself in a two-decade career and multiple NBA championships won with the Lakers. Fans and sportswriters alike believe that Bryant is one of the greatest athletes currently playing in the NBA. They mention his name alongside retired basketball greats like Wilt Chamberlain and Michael Jordan.

# Young and Talented

**K**obe Bean Bryant was born on August 23, 1978, in Philadelphia, Pennsylvania. He has two older sisters, Shaya and Sharia. His parents are Pamela and Joe Bryant.

Basketball runs in the Bryant family. Kobe's father was a professional basketball player in the 1970s and 1980s. He was a power forward for the Philadelphia 76ers, San Diego Clippers (now L.A. Clippers), and Houston Rockets. Young Kobe used to watch his father's games on television. He would wear a team uniform that matched his dad's and pretend that he was playing the game, too.

## QUICK FACT

Kobe Bryant's parents chose his first name from the expensive type of beef they saw at a Japanese restaurant. His middle name is a nod to his father's nickname, Jellybean.

This photo of Kobe and his parents was taken in 2000, after the Los Angeles Lakers won the NBA championship.

# Growing Up in Italy

When Kobe was six, his father moved the family to Italy so that he could play professional basketball in the Italian league. In Italy, Joe Bryant flourished and was a high-scoring player. Kobe remembers that when he watched his dad's games, fans sang songs about him.

Kobe started playing sports at a young age. He played soccer as well as basketball before he decided to concentrate on basketball. He played basketball as a club sport. At one point, his club was the youth league of the professional team that his father played for. Their uniforms even matched!

> **QUICK FACT**
>
> There are athletes on both sides of Bryant's family. His mother's brother is Chubby Cox, who played professional basketball in the 1970s and 1980s.

Joe Bryant sometimes brought Kobe along to watch him practice with his team. By the time he was thirteen, Kobe had gotten so good at basketball that he could beat some of Joe's teammates in games of one-on-one!

Bryant has said that the style of basketball he learned to play growing up in Italy is similar to how the game was played in the NBA in the 1950s and 1960s. He thinks this style focuses on the fundamentals of the game. He says that kids growing up in the United States in his generation were taught what he thinks of as a flashier style of play. When he returned to the United States, Bryant became determined to add these stylish moves to his already great skills. He called this "putting icing on the cake."

> **QUICK FACT**
>
> Kobe learned to speak Italian and learned to read books in Latin at his Italian schools.

Joe Bryant played on teams based in the Lazio, Calabria, Toscana, and Emilia-Romagna regions of Italy.

# From High School to the NBA

The Bryant family returned to the United States in 1991 and settled in Ardmore, Pennsylvania. Kobe Bryant had a hard time fitting in at first because his years living in Italy made him feel out of step with American culture and African American culture. Kobe was also a bit of a loner. As an adult, Bryant believes this is a positive trait because it forces him to stay true to himself.

As a teenager, Kobe suffered from Osgood-Schlatter disease. This is a condition that causes knee pain. It happens most often to teens during their peak growth years because quick growth puts a strain on their muscles, bones, and tendons. Sports like basketball are hard on these body parts, too. Bryant has said that he had to work through a lot of pain during this time.

In 1992, Kobe entered Lower Merion High School, where he joined the basketball team. He was an outstanding player and the team was state champion all four years that Kobe played. People were so eager to see the Lower Merion team play that tickets to their games sold out. During his senior year in high school, Kobe was named the Naismith national player of the year. He finished his high school career as the all-time leading scorer in southeastern Pennsylvania high school basketball history. It would prove to be just a taste of greatness to come.

Because Bryant was such a great high-school player, there were many colleges that would have been happy to recruit him. Although he devoted much of his time to basketball, Kobe was also a good student, with good grades and SAT scores. At one point, Kobe was considering going to Duke University because the school was known for its academics as well as its athletics.

## QUICK FACT

Players no longer go directly from high school to the NBA. In 2005, the rules were changed so that players must be at least nineteen and one year out of high school before they can be drafted.

Kobe helps the Lower Merion High School team defeat Chester High School in the Pennsylvania Interscholastic Athletic Association District I Finals in 1996.

Kobe had his eye on the NBA, though. In fact, because of his father's past ties to the team, he was able to start working out with the 76ers while he was still playing for his high school team! During his senior year, he decided to put himself up for the NBA Draft instead of

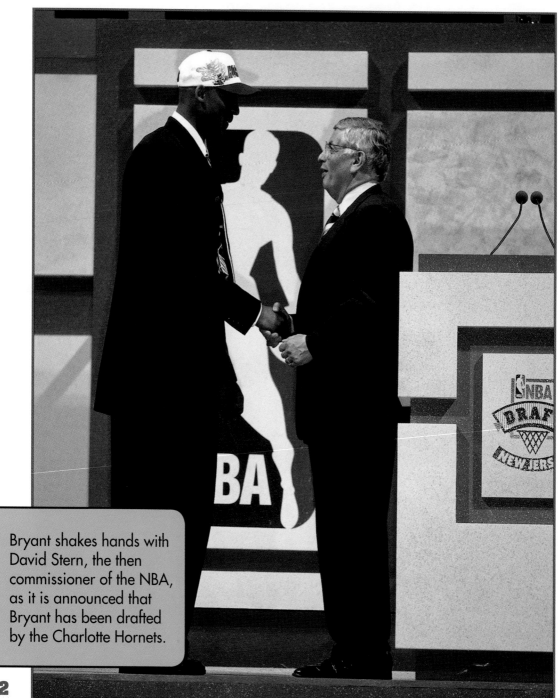

Bryant shakes hands with David Stern, the then commissioner of the NBA, as it is announced that Bryant has been drafted by the Charlotte Hornets.

playing at the college level. He stood in front of the press at his high school and announced, "I've decided to skip college and take my talents to the NBA." He was only the sixth player ever to go to the NBA straight out of high school.

The Charlotte Hornets picked Kobe in the 1996 draft, but then traded him to the Los Angeles Lakers for Vlade Divac. Bryant was only seventeen when he signed with the Lakers. Because he was not legally an adult, his parents had to cosign his contract with the team!

# The L.A. Lakers

**W**hen Kobe Bryant began playing with the Los Angeles Lakers in 1996, he was the youngest player ever to appear in an NBA game. During his rookie season, Bryant said that he thought fans liked him because they saw him as an underdog that they wanted to succeed.

Early on in his rookie season, Bryant often saw limited play, only coming off the bench after guards Eddie Jones or Nick Van Exel. As the season went along, he started to get more minutes on the court. He proved his skills to Lakers fans by winning the 1997 Slam Dunk Contest. This is a competition held during the NBA All-Star Weekend. He was also picked for the NBA All-Rookie second team. Each year, head coaches honor the league's best rookies by naming them to the NBA All-Rookie team.

Even in his rookie season, Bryant demonstrated flashes of showmanship. Here he is scoring during a 1997 game against the Detroit Pistons.

In the 1997–1998 season, the Lakers were 61–21 for the year. While they made the play-offs, they lost to the Utah Jazz in the Western Conference finals. In that same season, Bryant was chosen for the All-Star team. In fact, he became the youngest player to start in an All-Star game.

Bryant goes for a dunk during his very first All-Star Game on February 8, 1998.

The 1998–1999 season was shortened to fifty games due to an NBA lockout. A lockout happens when there is an ongoing dispute between NBA team owners and the union that represents the NBA players. The Lakers were 31–19 for the season. Bryant averaged 19.9 points per game and made the All-Star team. The Lakers made the play-offs again but lost to the San Antonio Spurs in the Western Conference semifinals.

In these early seasons, Bryant felt he was being underused. His career would begin to transform when the Lakers brought on Phil Jackson as head coach for the 1999–2000 season. Jackson had famously coached the Chicago Bulls to six NBA championships, and it was hoped that he could bring out greatness in the Lakers. Jackson's coaching made great use of the triangle offense. This is an offensive strategy that uses the center, a forward, and a guard to form a triangle that creates spacing between players to allow passing that is responsive to the opposing team's moves.

## Ups and Downs

In the 1999–2000 season, Kobe Bryant came into his own as one of the best shooting guards in the NBA. He led his team in assists and steals. That season, he made the All-Star team, as well as the All-Defensive team and the All-NBA team. These teams recognize the best players in the NBA.

As members of the Lakers, Bryant and center Shaquille O'Neal were the foundation of coach Phil Jackson's

### QUICK FACT

Bryant gave himself the nickname Black Mamba. He got the idea from the *Kill Bill* movies, in which this is an assassin's code name. A black mamba is a venomous snake.

### QUICK FACT

Shaquille O'Neal has said that his and Bryant's teamwork was the "greatest one-two punch— little man, big man—in the history of the game."

While Bryant and Shaquille O'Neal did not always see eye-to-eye personally, both were key in coach Phil Jackson's triangle defense strategy.

triangle offense strategy. This strategy immediately began to pay off for the team.

The Lakers finished the regular season with 67 wins and 15 losses. During the play-offs, Bryant proved himself a great clutch player, helping the Lakers win their first NBA championship since 1988.

The Lakers continued to be a winning team in the 2000–2001 season, with 56 wins and 26 losses. They won the NBA championship for the second year in a row. Bryant was named to both the All-NBA second team and the NBA's All-Defensive second team.

The Lakers had another great year in the 2001–2002 season, this time with 58 wins and 24 losses. Bryant was honored for his great performance by being named to the All-NBA first team, the All-Defensive second team, and the All-Star Game MVP. The Lakers won the NBA finals for the third year in a row. Winning three championships in a row is called a "three-peat."

Bryant poses with his teammates (left to right) Rick Fox, Lindsey Hunter, and Shaquille O'Neal after the Lakers swept the New Jersey Nets in the 2002 NBA championships.

In the 2002–2003 season, the Lakers were 50–32, but they were defeated in the second round of the play-offs. Bryant made the All-NBA first team and the All-NBA Defensive first team.

Although the Lakers were winning, tension was beginning to rise between Bryant, Jackson, and O'Neal. Jackson ordered Bryant not to "pull a Michael Jordan" by taking over the ball during games. Bryant and O'Neal played well together, but they did not get along because they had such different personalities and playing styles. O'Neal thought Bryant was trying to rack up individual honors rather than playing for the team. Bryant thought O'Neal relied more on his size than his skills as a player. The two began to dislike one another.

Early on, Bryant developed a reputation for being aloof, or seeming cold and distant to other people. He later said that he was so excited to be playing basketball that he did not think about hanging out with his teammates or talking to fans. It was only after he was asked about his attitude that he started to think about himself as a public figure and how what he does both on and off the court makes an impression on people. He began to make the effort to connect with fans off the court.

Bryant signs autographs for young fans at a special holiday party that the Lakers held for local military families in 2004.

# Controversy

In the summer of 2003, Bryant was accused of assaulting a woman in a hotel room. Bryant made a settlement with the woman and all charges were eventually dropped, but the incident led to him losing most of his sponsorships and many fans. He had to work to regain the public's trust.

Bryant's legal problems meant that he missed games in the 2003–2004 season because he had to appear in court. The Lakers had a 56–26 season and reached the NBA Finals, but they lost the championship to the Detroit Pistons. Bryant was once again named to the All-NBA first team and the All-Defensive first team.

Bryant's contract with the Lakers was up at the end of the 2003–2004 season. There were rumors that he was going to move to the L.A. Clippers, but he re-signed with the Lakers on a seven-year contract. In part because O'Neal found Bryant so difficult to work with, he then asked to be traded and moved to the Miami Heat. Coach Phil Jackson, who did not want O'Neal to change teams and thought O'Neal was easier to work with than Bryant, decided to take a break from coaching.

The departures of O'Neal and Jackson brought Bryant more attention as the Lakers' star player. He continued to play well, being picked for the All-NBA third team in the 2004–2005 season. The Lakers struggled as a team, however, and ended the 2004–2005 season with a 34–48 record.

## QUICK FACT

Opposing teams often assigned a player whose only mission was to shadow Bryant to keep him from scoring.

# Bouncing Back

Coach Phil Jackson returned to the Lakers for the 2005–2006 season. The Lakers were 45–37 in the 2005–2006 season, but they lost to the Phoenix Suns in the NBA play-offs. Bryant was happy Jackson had returned, and he

Bryant gets past Chris Bosh and Mike James of the Toronto Raptors to score during his famous "81 Game" on January 22, 2006.

had one of the best seasons of his career. He was named All-NBA first team and All-Defensive first team.

On January 22, 2006, Bryant played one of his most famous games. He scored 81 points in the Lakers' 122–104 win over the Toronto Raptors. Wilt Chamberlain's historic 100-point game in 1962 was the only performance to top Bryant's. When asked about the "81 Game," Bryant said, "I had worked extremely hard the summer before that. That game was the culmination of days and days of hard work."

Bryant was the top NBA scorer in the 2006–2007 season, with an average of 31.6 points per game. He had four straight games in which he scored 50 or more

Kia Motors president Alex Fedorak presents Bryant with his first MVP Award at a press conference on May 6, 2008.

points and there were ten total games in which he scored at least 50 points. This is another record that is topped only by Wilt Chamberlain. Bryant was named to the All-NBA first team, the NBA All-Defensive first team, and was the All-Star Game MVP. The Lakers were 42–40 for the season. Again they found themselves defeated in the play-offs by the Phoenix Suns.

During the summer of 2007, there were reports that Bryant was asking to be traded away from the Lakers. He did not like the direction that management was taking with building the team. He later changed his mind and said that he still dreamed of playing for the Lakers for the rest of his career. He began to work on his relationships with his teammates, trying to show more leadership and acting less aloof.

The Lakers were 57–25 in the 2007–2008 season. They made it to the NBA Finals but lost to the Boston Celtics. Bryant once again made the All-NBA first team and the All-Defensive NBA first team. His increasing leadership on the court helped him earn his first league MVP award.

# Breaking Records

**P**laying basketball in the Olympics was a lifelong dream of Bryant's. In 2000, he was asked to replace the injured Grant Hill, but he did not because he did not feel he had time to prepare. He could not play in the 2004 Olympics because he was dealing with legal problems from the assault charge.

In 2008 Bryant was ready and able to play at the Beijing Olympics. He helped the United States bring home the gold medal for men's basketball. Bryant played for the United States again at the London Olympics in 2012. The United States men's basketball team once again won the gold medal.

## QUICK FACT

When he played at the 2008 Olympics, Bryant asked to be assigned to play against the opposing team's best scorer.

Bryant helped Team USA bring home the gold for basketball in the 2008 Olympics in Beijing, China. Here he is driving against Felizardo Ambrosio of Angola.

## An NBA MVP

The Lakers continued to excel in the 2008–2009 season. Pau Gasol, whose skills complemented Bryant's, joined the team. One of Gasol's strengths was assists. He was especially good at grabbing rebounds of shots that Bryant missed.

Bryant was not missing many shots, though! In a February 2, 2009, win against the New York Knicks, he scored 61 points. It was the most single-game points scored by a player that season.

On February 15, Bryant played in the 2009 All-Star Game and was named its MVP. Throughout the rest of the season, Bryant met or surpassed scoring records. He became the youngest player to score 23,000 points in his career, beating a record set by Wilt Chamberlain in 1967. On February 20, Bryant reached twentieth place for all-time career points. By the season's end he was in fifteenth place!

The Lakers finished the season with a 65–17 record. Once again the team won the NBA championship. Bryant was named the NBA Finals MVP after averaging a stellar 32.4 points per game in the series.

Bryant and Pau Gasol were teammates from 2008 to 2014. The two players demonstrated great teamwork together.

Bryant broke his right index finger in December 2009. This meant he had to play most of the 2009–2010 season wearing a splint on that finger. The injury also meant he had to change the way he used his fingers to follow through on shots. It did not affect how accurate he was at making shots, though.

Bryant hit several milestones in the 2009–2010 season. By the season's end, he had moved up to twelfth place for all-time career points. He became the youngest player to reach 25,000 career points. He was chosen for the All-NBA first team, the NBA All-Defensive first team, and the All-Star Game.

The Lakers were 57–25 in the 2009–2010 season and won the NBA championship for the second year in a row. Bryant was the NBA Finals MVP for the second year in a row, too.

## Personal Bests

The Lakers had 57 wins and 25 losses in the 2010–2011 season. They hoped to have another "three-peat" of NBA championships but were knocked out in the semifinals by the Dallas Mavericks.

Bryant hit still more personal bests as a player during this season. He once again played in the All-Star Game and was chosen as its MVP for the fourth time. He also became the youngest player to score 26,000 career points, moving up to sixth place on the NBA career-scoring list.

> ## QUICK FACT
>
> Film director Spike Lee made a documentary about Bryant in 2009. It is called *Kobe Doin' Work.*

> ## QUICK FACT
>
> Bryant gave himself the nickname Vino. This is the Italian word for "wine." He chose the nickname to indicate that he is getting better as he ages, as wine is said to do.

In 2010, the Lakers won the NBA championship and Bryant was named the Finals MVP. Here he holds the trophies for both achievements.

Coach Phil Jackson left the Lakers after the 2010–2011 season and was replaced by Mike Brown for the 2011–2012 season. There was an NBA lockout at the beginning of the season. The lockout delayed the start of the season, so only 66 games were played, rather than 82.

Bryant scored 23 points during this February 10, 2011, game against the Boston Celtics, leading the Lakers to a 92–86 victory.

The Lakers were 41–25 in this shortened season. Bryant hoped to win the sixth NBA championship of his career. Doing so would have given Bryant as many championships as his hero Michael Jordan, who had played for the Chicago Bulls in the 1990s. The Oklahoma City Thunder defeated the Lakers during the play-offs, however.

Bryant did hit milestones during the 2011–2012 season, though. He was chosen for his fourteenth All-Star Game. He became the youngest player to score 29,000 career points. Bryant also passed Shaquille O'Neal to reach fifth place on the NBA career-scoring list.

Bryant played in his fourteenth All-Star Game in 2012. He scored a record-setting 280 career All-Star Game points during this contest.

# An All-Star Player

The 2012–2013 season got off to a bad start. The team lost four of their first five games, after which coach Mike Brown was fired. Some fans hoped Phil Jackson would return from retirement again, but the team's management chose Mike D'Antoni as the new coach. Laker Steve Nash

The Lakers acquired Steve Nash *(left)* and Dwight Howard *(right)* for the 2012–2013 season. Howard and Bryant did not get along, which caused the team to struggle throughout the season.

had already played under D'Antoni with the Phoenix Suns. Bryant knew D'Antoni, too. He had been a basketball player in Italy when Bryant's father had played there.

D'Antoni coached the Lakers to use the Princeton offense. This strategy emphasizes constant passing and requires teamwork from everyone on the court. It took time for the team to adjust to it and often led to clashes between Bryant and his teammate Dwight Howard, who transferred to the Houston Rockets after the end of that season.

Toward the end of the season, Bryant injured his Achilles tendon. He missed the last two games of the season and needed surgery and several months of recovery afterward. Before getting injured, Bryant had played in that season's All-Star Game, was named to the All-NBA first team, and reached fourth place on the NBA career-scoring list.

While Bryant recovered from surgery to his Achilles tendon, he used Twitter to document his progress for his fans. In interviews, he said his injury was healing ahead of schedule. His trainers believed he would need a full year to heal, but Bryant returned to the court after only seven months. He still missed the beginning of the 2013–2014 season, though. His first game back was on December 8, in a loss against the Toronto Raptors. Bryant's return did not last long, though. On December 17, in only his sixth game of the season, Bryant broke his left knee and had to sit out the rest of the season.

Bryant continued to be sidelined by injuries for much of the 2014–2015 season. It was his nineteenth with the Lakers. This tied him with the Utah Jazz's John Stockton for most seasons with an NBA team. Bryant assures fans that he plans to finish his career with the Lakers, and when he does yet another record will have been set.

# Kobe Off the Court

## QUICK FACT

Bryant loves sharks. He says that he would like to go diving in a shark cage after he retires.

**A**long with basketball, Kobe Bryant is also interested in business. He has ongoing sponsorships with Turkish Air, Lenovo, Hublot, Panini, and Nike. He started a company called Kobe Inc. so that he can invest in businesses outside of advertising for them.

After all of his success, Bryant is interested in helping others through charity work. He works with a tutoring program called After-School All-Stars. This is a program that helps kids in Los Angeles schools.

Bryant got to meet President Barack Obama in 2010 while doing a volunteer project for the Boys and Girls Club in Washington, D.C.

# Kobe's Family

Bryant met Vanessa Laine in 1999 while on the set for a video shoot for a rap album that he had recorded. They married in 2001. In 2011, Vanessa filed for divorce, but in 2013 the couple announced on Facebook that they had reconciled. This means that they got back together.

The Bryants have two daughters. Natalia was born in 2003. Gianna was born in 2006. Bryant has said that Natalia's personality is more like Vanessa's but that Gianna is super-competitive, just like he is.

Bryant says that spending part of his childhood in Italy inspired a curiosity about the world in him. During the summers, he and Vanessa travel all over the world with their daughters because they think it is important to

Bryant poses with his wife, Vanessa *(left)*, and their children, Natalia *(center)* and Gianna *(right)*.

expose them to different cultures. For himself, if he has time in his schedule when he travels to "away" games he sometimes sits in on a college class. He has done this at Boston College and the University of Miami.

# A Lakers Legend

Because he is an experienced player, Bryant acts as a leader to his fellow Lakers. He knows what it is like to be a rookie and he has tried to mentor younger players, such as small forward Wesley Johnson. It is a role he takes seriously.

He also says that it is important to keep the team motivated to work hard. Bryant is a big believer in the importance of hard work. As a leader, he sees it as part of his job to demonstrate discipline as well as to expect it from his teammates. He says that many people shy away from

Bryant takes his leadership role in the Lakers seriously. He likes to give support and advice to newer teammates, such as Jeremy Lin (left) and Nick Young (center).

## QUICK FACT

Besides practice and taking care of himself, Bryant makes it a priority to study the game footage. He calls this his "homework."

pushing people to do better because they worry about being liked. He knows that in the long run his teammates appreciate him for the success brought on by the hard work he pushed them to do.

Bryant signed a two-year contract extension with the Lakers in November 2013. This means that two years were added to the contract he already had. The contract is worth $48.5 million. Bryant had said that he will likely retire from basketball when the contract is up in 2016. He is already ranked by many sportswriters as one of the best players in NBA history, but he would like to break more records before he ends his career. He hopes to leave the game on a high note, leaving fans as excited as the day he joined the NBA.

**1978:** Kobe Bean Bryant is born on August 23 in Philadelphia, Pennsylvania.

**1984:** Bryant's father moves the family to Italy.

**1991:** The Bryants return to the United States. They settle in Ardmore, Pennsylvania.

**1992–1996:** Kobe plays basketball for the Lower Merion high-school team and attracts national attention for his skills.

**1996:** Bryant announces that he will not go to college but go straight from high school to the NBA. He joins the Los Angeles Lakers.

**1999:** Meets Vanessa Laine. The couple would go on to marry in 2001.

**2000:** The Lakers win the NBA championship.

**2001:** The Lakers win the NBA championship.

**2002:** The Lakers win the NBA championship for the third year in a row. This is known as a "three-peat."

**2003:** Bryant's daughter Natalia is born on January 19.

**2006:** Bryant's daughter Gianna is born on May 1.

**2008:** Bryant is named the NBA MVP for the 2007–2008 season.

**2009:** The Lakers win the NBA championship. Bryant is the NBA Finals MVP.

**2010:** The Lakers win the NBA championship. Bryant is the NBA Finals MVP.

**2014:** Bryant becomes the fourth NBA player ever to reach 32,000 career points on November 18.

**Kareem Abdul-Jabbar (1947–)** had a career that spanned from 1969 to 1989. He played center for the Milwaukee Bucks and the Lakers. He won one NBA championship with the Bucks and five with the Lakers. He was a six-time MVP and a nineteen-time NBA All-Star. Abdul-Jabbar still ranks first in all-time points, field goals, and minutes played.

**Larry Bird (1956–)** played forward with the Boston Celtics from 1979 to 1992. He won three NBA championships. He was a twelfve-time NBA All-Star and a three-time MVP. Bird was a member of the gold medal–winning "Dream Team" in the 1992 Summer Olympics.

**Earvin "Magic" Johnson (1959–)** played point guard for the Lakers from 1979 to 1991 and in 1996. He won five NBA championships and was a three-time MVP. This twelve-time All-Star ranks first in all-time per-game assists. Johnson won a gold medal in men's basketball in the 1992 Summer Olympics.

**Hakeem Olajuwon (1963–)** played center for the Houston Rockets from 1984 to 2001 and the Toronto Raptors in the 2001–2002 season. Nicknamed "the Dream," he led the Rockets to NBA championships in 1994 and 1995. He became the first player to win the Most Valuable Player, Finals MVP, and Defensive Player of the Year in the same season in 1994.

**Michael Jordan (1963–)** was a shooting guard and small forward who played for the Chicago Bulls from 1984 to 1993 and 1995 to 1998 and for the Washington Wizards from 2001 to 2003. He was a fourteen-time All-Star and a five-time MVP. Jordan led the Bulls to six NBA championships and was a two-time gold medalist in men's basketball (1984 and 1992).

## Shaquille O'Neal (1972–) had a career that spanned

from 1992 to 2011. He played center for the Orlando Magic, Los Angeles Lakers, Miami Heat, Cleveland Cavaliers, and the Boston Celtics. His huge size made it hard for other teams to defend against him. He was a fifteen-time NBA All-Star. He won four NBA championships, three with the Lakers and one with the Heat.

## Tim Duncan (1976–) led the San Antonio Spurs to NBA

championships in 1999, 2003, 2005, 2007, and 2014. Known for his unflashy style and low-key personality, Duncan was named the MVP in 2002 and 2003, as well as the Finals MVP in 1999, 2003, and 2005.

## LeBron James (1984–) is a forward who debuted with

the Cleveland Cavaliers in 2003, moved to the Miami Heat in 2010, and returned to the Cavaliers in 2014. He won two NBA championships for the Heat. He is a four-time MVP, ten-time All-Star, and a two-time Summer Olympic gold medalist in men's basketball (2008 and 2012).